MY PADDED
PICTURE DICTIONARY
BOOK

balloon · hat · radio · candles · card · cake · streamer · present · party bag

This book includes fun, brightly coloured illustrations of everyday scenes, combined with words relating to images and objects in each scene. Use the combination of the scenes, objects, images and words to teach your child picture and word recognition.

toothbrushes

soap

taps

towels

sink

toilet

slippers

mirror

sponge

duck

bath

mat

kite

hat

spade

sand
castle

bucke

ship

lighthouse

boat

seagull

crab

top hat

ringmaster

juggler

balloon

horse

clown

blackboard

crayons

picture

brush

paint

horse

cow

sty

pig

sheep

hay

tractor

dog

bird

monkey

alligator

gorilla

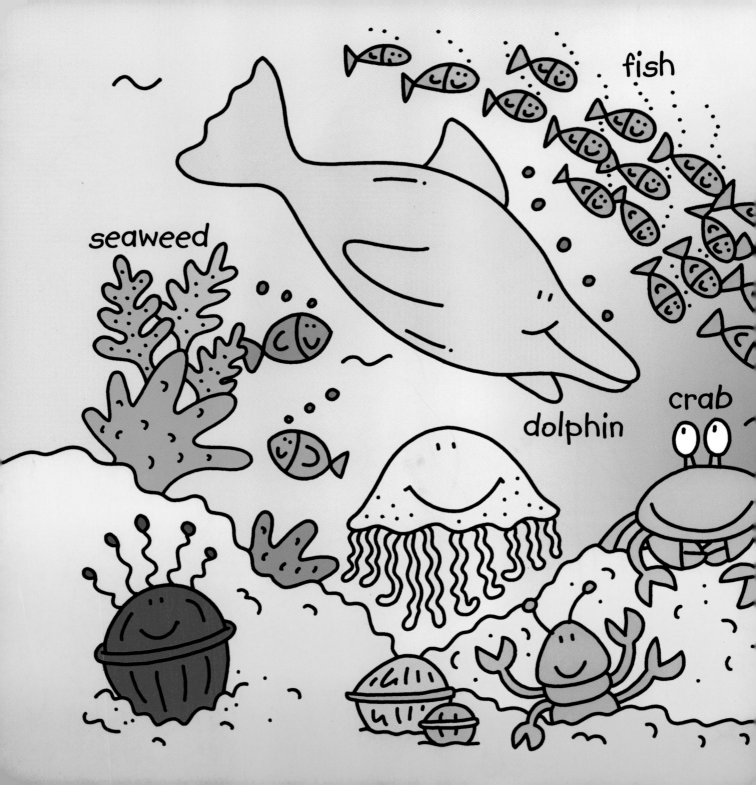

fish

seaweed

dolphin

crab

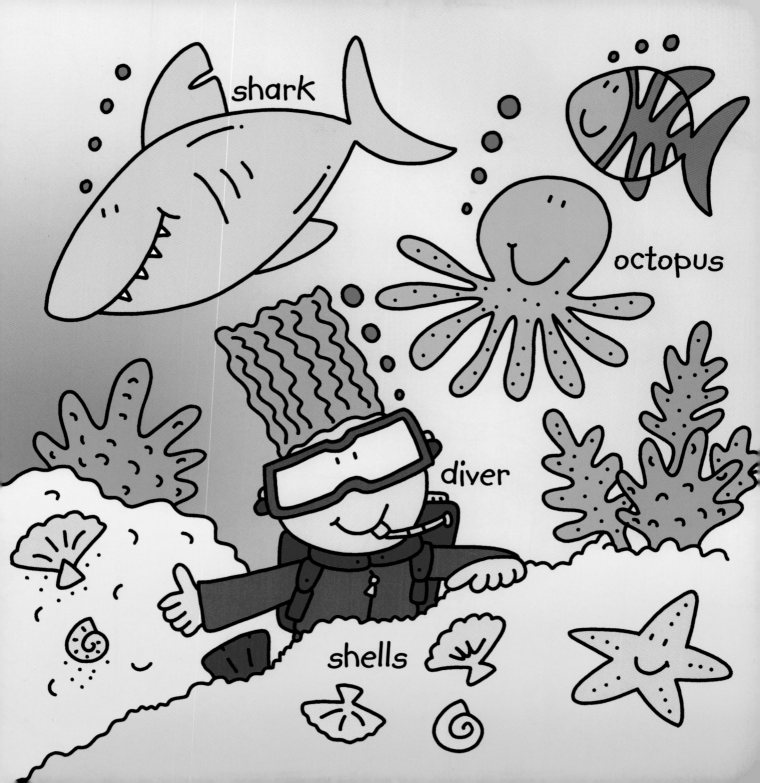

radio

card

streamer

party bag

kite

boy

bike

bird

flowers